The
Town Mouse
and the
Country Mouse

Retold by Susan Akass

Illustrated by Tony Ross

Once upon a time
a mouse had a little hole in a tree.
'I am Country Mouse,' he said.

In the town a mouse had
a little hole in a house.
'I am Town Mouse,' he said.

One day Town Mouse said,
'I will go to see Country Mouse.'
He ran to the country.

'What do you eat in the country?'
said Town Mouse.

'I eat corn,' said Country Mouse.

'But I don't like corn,'
said Town Mouse.

'I don't like the country,'
said Town Mouse.
'We will go to my house in the town,'
he said.

Town Mouse and Country Mouse
went to the town.

'What do you eat in the town?'
said Country Mouse.
'I eat cheese,' said Town Mouse.
'I like cheese,' said Country Mouse.

Town Mouse and Country Mouse
jumped up on the table.
'Yum, yum,' said Country Mouse.
'I like it here in the town.'

'Get down, get down!'
said Town Mouse.
'I can see a cat.'

The cat jumped up on the table.
'Help! Help!' said Town Mouse.
'I will go to my hole.'

'I don't like the town,'
said Country Mouse.
'I will go to my hole in the country.'
And off he went.